Make Money Teaching Online

3rd EDITION

THE SERIES!

DANI BABB, PhD

Make Money Teaching Online. The Series!
3rd edition

Copyright © Dani Babb, Phd

Contents

Part 11:
Must-Have Technologies
for Online Educators

"Education is not preparation for life; education is life itself."

~John Dewey

Teaching online is exactly what it sounds like: an online, remote job. While this is common today, when I co-authored the first edition of this book, it was highly unusual. As with many online jobs, there are essentials and nonessentials, and one of the essentials is technology—lots of it! Technology should make you more efficient, make your job easier and your overall job satisfaction higher. Technology not only is required to actually do the job, but much of it is required to keep your hectic life organized while meeting many demanding deadlines, scheduling calls, and reminding yourself of important to-do items.

This section of the series will start off with technology to make your life easier, and end with insights from Dr. Jena Hinds on taking a mindful and differentiated approach to online and hybrid courses. Dr. Hinds runs sessions for us in technology and for some of our University clients, and truly has the art of the flipped classroom down, as well (which you will come to appreciate as you do more live sessions!).

The payoff for implementing some of these ideas is immeasurable, but the most important task is first to get hired; so get what you need to do the job, then get the job, and then get what you need to do the job better so you can maximize your earnings! Let's begin with what you absolutely must have to do your job. That, after all, is most important.

Internet Access

When it comes to Internet access, speed isn't everything; it's the only thing. You cannot afford to waste time uploading files, downloading files, and opening websites when that time could be put to more practical use. You also need extreme reliability. The extra cost of high-speed Internet access in your home will easily pay for itself if you teach just one online course per year. Long ago, some schools would reimburse you for it; not so anymore, unless you are a full time employee – then it may be an option. Also, the cost of having high-speed Internet access is tax-deductible if you are earning income as an online professor (but ask your tax guy or gal to confirm)! I use a mesh network to ensure complete coverage throughout my home so I can work anywhere.

Computers

Of all the equipment in your home office, the most critical is the computer, and it needs to be a fast one. This means your computer must be able to take full advantage of the high-speed Internet access and must be capable of multitasking well enough that you aren't frustrated, nor are you waiting for your machine to catch up while you have 10 web browsers open and your email up constantly, recording videos and doing live chats. This is one case where the speed of your computer truly will make an impact on how fast you are capable of doing your work. You will want a fast processor, plenty of memory, a good monitor (or two), and a comfortable keyboard and mouse.

Some of you may choose to work off a laptop computer (I do some of the time), while others may prefer a desktop. Be sure you have a reliable machine. You cannot afford to have your computer crash or be bogged down with software you don't need, and I highly recommend a redundant computer in case you lose a drive and need to wait for Amazon to deliver another one. If you are not computer savvy, you might want to invest in a service where you get 24/7 technical support. My personal preference switched a decade ago from Windows-based computers to Macs, as the integration with my phone is seamless and allows me to work much faster. Whatever you decide, make sure you can support it and you feel you know the system well.

Be sure that you have antivirus software, a firewall (hardware or software, or preferably, both) and every browser imaginable. Sometimes some system at a school won't work on Chrome, but will work on some outdated version of Firefox. It sounds crazy, but it is sadly true. Also, if things do not work reliably and you're on a Microsoft or Firefox browser, consider using Chrome consistently. Some of the more recent LMS updates have been engineered for Chrome.

You should also consider having a laptop even if you prefer to work off a desktop. Even with the best computer equipment, you cannot control how often the Internet may go down in your home. Short of a hurricane that wipes out power in your city, there is no reason you cannot take your laptop to the nearest coffee shop and continue to do your work.

Backups

Backups are the second most critical item, next to Internet access, that you will need for your computer. You absolutely must have backups. Some online systems store student grades on their systems; others don't and you must keep spreadsheets and records. Certainly you will build a database of discussion responses and videos. I like TextExpander for recurring notes that expand into comments into the LMS or student papers, announcements and the like that I can organize by school. I also use Time Machine software and have hourly backups, plus nightly backups using CCCloner. These are my Mac-based tools, and of course there are even more for Windows-based machines. You can also use cloud storage like Microsoft and Google's solutions for backups.

The key with backups is consistency and making certain you have at least one copy off-site in case someone steals your computers. Make sure your backups are working and make sure you do them often. This will save you tremendous headaches should something become corrupted, you get hit with a virus, have hard-drive failure, or worse.

Organization Systems and PDAs

It doesn't matter whether you use Outlook, your iPhone calendar, Google calendar, or some off-the-wall product you got free online, but use something to remind yourself when to submit attendance at certain schools, when various programs start, when to set up new classes, when to email your bosses, and various other recurring tasks. Make sure you can schedule recurring appointments, and if you can categorize, it will make doing so even easier.

Now, this brings up yet another requirement. Whatever you choose, it *must* synchronize to a smart phone. If you teach for more than a few schools, watch out for Android limitations on the number of email addresses you can add. I was (am) a big Android fan, but had to move to Apple because they do not limit how many email addresses you can have. With 10 personal accounts alone, Android wasn't an option for me and it may not be for some of you, either. With mobile applications of some of the LMSs, you can login and work from your smartphone, too. I personally like adding every email address at every school into my phone as it allows me to check them under the "all mail" option at one time, and reply to students and bosses as items come in. Some schools do not allow for mobile access, but I have found 90% do. Others will require you to use the Outlook app, and sometimes even require re-authentication on a daily basis.

Multifactor Authentication

One of the changes that has occurred since the last edition of this book is the heavy use of multifactor authentication, or MFA. Likely any school you work for will require some sort of double authentication method. Some schools will require reauthentication only if you are on a new device, and other more aggressive schools will require it every single day even from the same device. Be sure your smartphone can handle authenticator apps. While it was an irritating additional step the first few places that rolled it out, it's commonplace now, even for the most casual schools. If you travel a lot, I recommend that one of your phone numbers attached to your account is a Google Voice number so you can receive text messages even if your access is a little unreliable while traveling.

Voice Over Internet Protocol (VoIPs)

VoIP was a "nice to have" in the old days when we had to pay for every long distance phone call, but since most home landline providers offer free long distance now, it is less of an issue. I recommend a VoIP service (like Google) and also a landline in case Internet is out. With my students and bosses, I Skype, FaceTime and Google Chat.

Comfortable and Ergonomic Workstation Setups

You will be on your computer a lot. Have a comfortable, ergonomic workstation environment and save your wrists and hands. I like the Microsoft 5000 old school keyboard that I connect to my Mac, which I believe quite literally saved my wrists from surgery.

PDF Converters

Adobe's Portable Document Format (PDF) has become the de facto standard for sharing documents and information. Even official documents are being sent online this way. PDFs are less difficult to tamper with than Word or Excel documents, for instance, and most people are able to view them on their equipment. PDF readers are free online, and most universities will share information this way. A PDF converter lets you take, for instance, a Word file and save it as a PDF file, and vice versa. This lets you manipulate PDF files to sign contracts and easily send them back; it also lets you save, for instance, a Word test file into a PDF that students can't copy and paste from. This software has a multitude of uses and is relatively inexpensive. I like the paid Adobe PDF software because I can combine PDFs from multiple files into one (many schools require uploading your documents like this into their job application systems).

If you get faculty contracts that need to be signed and sent back, oftentimes just having them on your smartphone allows you to markup the file and return it right away. I like this for efficiency.

Printers

Even though you're teaching online, you'll find yourself printing student files or contracts. Many traditional schools will even have you scan, fax or mail in contracts. I would recommend asking around on the forum to find out what other professors use that are efficient. I like multifunction printers for their efficiency.

Backup Internet Providers

It might not be a bad idea to have a backup Internet provider, or to have hotspot capability on your smartphone in case your Internet goes out.

Uninterruptible Power Supply (UPS)

Don't run your PCs and laptops without an uninterruptible power supply (UPS). Not only will a UPS protect your equipment from power surges and lightning, but your system will continue running even in a power outage. I connect my cable modem and router to it, and can continue running without power as long as the cable provider keeps their equipment up.

Email Accounts

We used to recommend an email account with high in-box limitations, but that isn't an issue anymore. I can't think of even one school that wants you to email learners or administrators from your personal account. For all sorts of legal reasons, the schools want us to use their email accounts. This is one of many reasons the "all inbox" on our phones is so important. I also use CanaryMail, which supports synchronizing accounts across all of your devices and also supports multifactor authentication. Some schools will turn off third party support, so you may find some don't connect. It's an outstanding, very organized and intuitive service.

Office Suites

You will still need Microsoft Office, and Google won't usually cut it. Even if you convert everything to a Google Doc you will likely run into compatibility issues or problems with others opening your files. Schools that issue you a Microsoft account generally allow you to also download the Office suite, too. This shouldn't cost much, if anything, for you anymore.

Password Storage

You will be asked to remember more passwords than you ever thought imaginable in your life! This means you need a password and site storage utility. I personally like LastPass. Although some no longer recommend it due to some hacking incident in which actual passwords were *not* released, it took a bad PR hit and some no longer use it. I still find it invaluable.

Video Capability

There is no way around this. No matter how many hours we spend in our pajamas working (yeah, you!) you will have a day when you have to throw a professional looking jacket over the PJs, put on a headband and comb your eyebrows to do a video. Whether it's a welcome video, a meeting with a boss, a synchronous session, or an interview, someone at some point will want to see your face. Get a decent quality camera and microphone and make sure it works every now and again. There are some new technologies on the market that allow you to move the camera right to your eye but still see your screen.

Other Technology Recommendations from the Forums

Our forum members have some other great technology suggestions for efficiency and sanity! If you would like to read every comment, you can find it at www.facebook.com/groups/onlineprofessors.

Docusign account is used for contracts at more schools today than ever.

Evernote is for storing account information and remembering notes.

The website www.toggl.com is good for timing your work and seeing what universities are paying you.

Use SlideShare to upload lecture notes or slide presentations and embed them into Blackboard.

Office 365 enables you to access your data from any device.

TypeItIn is a great tool for repeating comments by clicking a button on your desktop.

High quality, noise canceling headphones are a necessity to block noise and keep the energy up.

Many online professors use multiple computer screens (this can come in very handy and save your neck from pain).

Standing desks or treadmill desks are useful if you want to keep moving and maintain ergonomics.

Ergonomic mouse or newer style replacement is helpful for hands and wrists.

Private Internet access, or a virtual private network, comes in handy to surf safely and securely while away.

Camtasia is a screen recording software tool that records what you're doing on your screen including audio, video, narration and description of slides you are developing or reviewing. This is a relatively painless way to create more engaging course content and share it with others.

Making Your Life Easier and the Students Happier

Most of the technologies mentioned thus far are designed for you to support your students, keep your life more organized, and make your business easier to manage. Some also help you look good to your bosses and make you more accessible. I recommend giving students many ways to contact you, while keeping it simple enough that you'll actually use them.

Here is what I offer to my own students. I am a tech nerd and I work on social media all of the time, so many of these are no big deal to me but understandably not for everyone:

- Twitter direct message questions to: @danibabb
- Email (school and personal for emergencies)
- Cell phone

- Whatsapp (international students appreciate this)
- iMessaging
- Google Hangouts

I selected the tools I am "on" most of the time so that it isn't an extra step each time I sit down to work. Also, these tools work on my smartphone, so they notify me when a text request comes in and I get a notification when a DM comes in on Twitter. Keep in mind the school may limit what you can use, though. Everyone will choose tools that are easiest and best for them. My goal, particularly teaching technology courses, is to be streamlined, efficient, and to be where the students already are – which usually means online browsing social media.

Setting Up a System to Support Flexibility and Travel

When you begin life as an adjunct, you may not be traveling much for work. As time goes on, you will find that this schedule picks up much more dramatically, particularly if you teach in doctoral programs that have residencies that you participate in. You'll want to set up a system that supports flexibility and travel. This means several things:

- Data that's easily transferable between laptop and desktop or automatically syncs (Dropbox, GDrive, SkyDrive, etc.).

- An organization method for your calendar that keeps you consistent and working well (I use Google Calendar and sync it to my smartphone).

- Smartphone with fast Internet access.

- A laptop with wireless capability.

- A straightforward, reliable laptop configured just like your desktop. This includes software you will use for only one class, but may need while traveling. Better to always install on both PCs than be traveling and realize you don't have what you need.

- A Virtual Private Network – though some schools are beginning to block these IP addresses from connecting to their networks. I like SmartVPN.

The key here is to understand how you do things, your lifestyle, what's important to you, and how you work. Then mimic this in your technology. You will find traveling a joy and far less stressful.

I would encourage you to share new technology tips in our forum and tell others what you find useful and productive. I learn of the best tools from my colleagues and many professors in our group are gurus with efficiency tools! Also, check the website often at www.facultyjobtools.com for the latest technology recommendations!

Now, most importantly, onto Dr. Hinds, who will share with us Online Tools to Help Make a More Mindful and Differentiated Approach to Online and Hybrid Courses!

Online Tools to Help Make a More Mindful and Differentiated Approach to Online and Hybrid Courses By: Jena Hinds, Ph.D.

The COVID-19 pandemic raised many global concerns and challenges among K–12 and higher education institutions. A particular problem was for teachers and instructors to continue doing classes online and most effectively. There was an urgency to move everything online, which caused stress and increased workload for teachers, faculty, and staff that were already struggling to balance teaching, research, and service obligations, as well as life outside of this (Houston et al., 2006; Veletsianos & Houlden, 2020). This was even more stressful for those with a learning disability and caused more anxiety and fear, which ultimately caused students to perform poorly (Hinds & Johns, 2023; Hinds & Sanchez, 2022). Now, with unexpected urgency, teachers, faculty, and staff went from face-to-face to teaching online from their own homes via Zoom or other platforms (Hodges, 2020). This was often done without the proper technical support to deliver an effective class lacking pedagogical content and knowledge (Angeli, 2005; Ching et al., 2018; Kali et al., 2011). With all of this, teachers were worried about providing each learner with the best educational resources and experience and the best student-parent relationships (Hodges, 2020). To do this, educators needed to explore options to help learners be more involved.

Even when the school went back to teaching in person, there were challenges in providing the best educational experience to all learners in various scenarios.

During this time, we were able to use and find a few learning platforms and online learning tools, such as Zoom, Google Drive, Padlet, Miro Board, Google Jamboard, and more. In this section, we will discuss some of these learning tools, the pros and cons we found with each of them, and how they may be beneficial to use in your online classroom to help encompass a more student-centered and engaging learning environment. When we share about a student-centered environment, it is meant to be perceived as less of a teacher lecture style of a class and more of a student-centered classroom with more student exploring and interacting with each other to discover and find answers.

As for a more mindful experience, we are sharing that the environment makes the student and the instructor feel less of stressed environment and more open to discussion, and the majority of students can feel comfortable responding, which in turn allows for more knowledge and skills to be retained (Hinds & Johns, 2023; Hinds & Sanchez, 2022). This also allows students to feel more open about asking questions and getting a better understanding of the course objectives (Hinds & Sanchez, 2022).

In this section, we review various tools to help engagement in an online classroom; it's important to note that no platform will fit every learning experience. Therefore, we suggest you explore the options and see which will fit each of your classes successfully.

Review of Platforms

An aspect of helping make an online classroom more of a mindful student-centered environment is adding online interactive tools to help improve the process and product in an educational environment. In this section, we will share a variety of online platforms that can be used, such as Zoom, OWL, Flipgrid, Mentimeter, Google Jamboard, Miro Board, Padlet, and Canva. We will share details about each of them, including some pros and cons. This will help you, as an educator, decide which ones may be useful tools for your classroom.

Zoom

Zoom is a platform that was used a little before the pandemic but even more in 2020 for K-12 and higher education institutions. Zoom is a cloud-based video conferencing service that features online meetings, group messaging, and secure recording of sessions (Inc, 2016). This platform is easy to use and provides students with access. It also gives the advantage of being able to record sessions and store them on a local drive, like a desktop, or a remote server, such as "the Cloud," for those who may have missed a class due to illness or other factors (Inc, 2016). Another benefit of Zoom is the ability to record who comes to the meeting and who leaves the meeting. The platform provides a high maximum participant capacity.

The downside of using Zoom is that individuals or institutions need to get the unlimited plan to have classes longer than 40 minutes, which adds to the cost a university faces with the pandemic. Another downside that some individuals have reported is "Zoom fatigue" or "Zoom exhaustion," where individuals feel tired from being on Zoom for long periods (Nesher Shoshan & Wehrt, 2022).

Another downside of using Zoom is that some teachers struggle to gauge student involvement and motivation and feel they still need to provide a personal experience when using an online interface. With this, it is essential to remember to take the time to get to know your students, be mindful of how they are feeling, be sure to incorporate interactive sessions where everyone is involved in the class discussion and with their classmates, and be sure to use strategies where a variety of students interact during a lecture so it's not just a teacher-centered classroom (Heflin, 2021).

OWL Labs

Another tool that schools and universities can use is the OWL, which gives video and audio experiences in a room with 360-degree coverage. This was a benefit when trying to teach students in class and online. The Owl video conferencing gives the feeling that the students who meet virtually are in the classroom, capturing all participants in the 360-degree field of view. The Owl follows the speaker around the room, where the students can see what is going on in the classroom, and it gives them a feeling of being an active participant when they are not necessarily present in person (Labs, 2023). The OWL is a user-friendly device that is easy to set up and use (Labs, 2023).

Some cons of having an OWL include the price, which ranges from $800 to $1800 (Labs, 2023). Another con that some may come across is the need for a stable internet connection for the Owl to work effectively, which could be an issue if someone has low bandwidth or an unreliable network environment. Although there is a 360-degree view, there is sometimes a lag when picking up the person's voice that is speaking in class.

Figure 1: This picture shows an individual videoing and using the OWL in a classroom. This shows that the individual online can visibly see the person talking and the presentation that is going on. (Labs, 2023)

Overall, the OWL is a great tool to add to classes, which will help accommodate students in person and virtually. This allows a classroom to be more interactive and allows all students to have the best interaction during a class.

Padlet

A third online tool that can be used for a more interactive online classroom is Padlet. Padlet is an online Post-it board where students, faculty, and staff can share what they want. The only thing needed is the Padlet link created by the instructor. This platform allows others to insert ideas anonymously or with their name attached to them. It is an easy platform to use, either in person or virtually. The user can pull up Padlet on their computer or smartphone and start writing where everyone with the code can view it. This is done live, so everyone sees your response immediately. Padlet can be used for any subject and allows the instructor to be creative, give immediate feedback, and use it for discussions amongst the students.

Some of the pros of using Padlet as an online interactive tool include that it is easy and user-friendly for a variety of ages, supports real-time posting, and supports a variety of content that can be used by a variety of professionals and educators. The use of Padlet for all ages makes it easy to teach how to get on the online tool, add content, and populate walls. Various forms of content can be added, such as text, videos, links, and images, allowing multiple means of action, engagement, and expression to increase interaction and engagement in an online classroom (Ali, 2021).

Figure 2: Padlet board. This is an example of what a Padlet board may look like. (Robinson, 2020)

Some of the cons of using Padlet include the fact that the free version of Padlet has limitations on how many active walls a user can have at once. It also limits the content that can be created and stored. The individual or institution would need to upgrade to the paid version for the additional walls, features, and storage to get unlimited walls ranging from $6.99 to $14.99 a month, a yearly subscription, or a school paying a starting rate of $1000 for unlimited teachers and students.

Overall, Padlet has been a great tool when doing in-person and virtual classes. The students were always interactive and enjoyed the ability to see their posts simultaneously.

Google Jamboard

O ther online tools that can be used and are free for users are Google Docs, Google Apps for Education, Spreadsheets, Presentations, and Google Jamboard (Amin, 2020; Khoiriyah et al., 2022). Jamboard is a whiteboard that is used to create and edit content by users. It can be used on a computer or via an app that can be downloaded for Android or iOS. Multiple users can use this tool at once and from any location. Jamboard is an interactive whiteboard where you can write, draw, and add colorful sticky notes and images. It is a graphic organizer with pictures, text, and so much more. The students really like using this because they can all work in synchronicity.

The pros of Google Jamboard include that the online platform is easy to use for students and is a way to have a more interactive class in real-time (Khoiriyah et al., 2022). Other students share that Google Jamboard is an easy way to study in groups, have discussions, and use mind mapping (Khoiriyah et al., 2022).

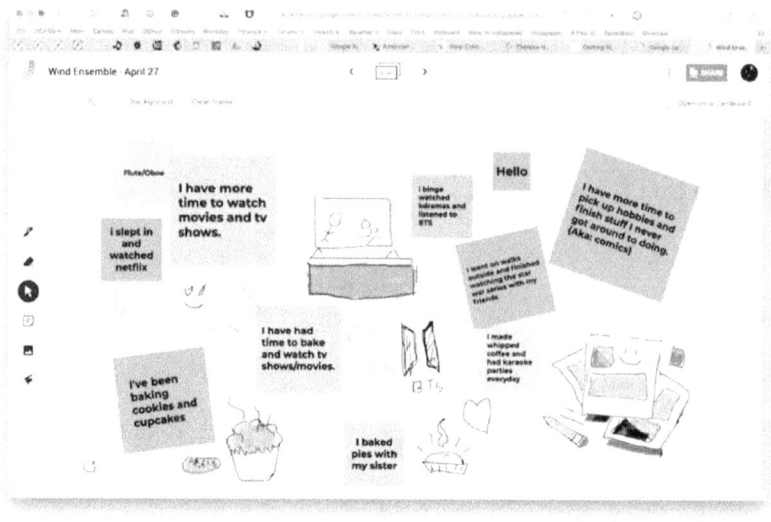

Figure 3: An example of Google Jamboard interactive posts (Navarro, 2021)

The cons of Google Jamboard include that individuals sometimes have glitches that interfere with the learning process (Khoiriyah et al., 2022). Another con is that there is a learning curve. Finally, another con is that Jamboard may not have every feature that some other online whiteboards may have, such as embedding videos and music (*Jamboard Reviews*, 2023).

Overall, Google Jamboard is a free tool that is easy to use and can help with student engagement. Although Google Jamboard is free, like some other individuals shared, it does not have all the features that other online whiteboards have.

Miro Board

Another educational tool that I personally use often is the Miro board. The Miro board is an online whiteboard that allows real-time collaboration between individuals and groups for educational purposes or projects. This online tool allows individuals to brainstorm, do projects, create visual presentations, organize ideas, and have an interactive experience with all individuals simultaneously (Johnson, 2022). Miro's interface is similar to a physical whiteboard but allows for various creative enhancements. Users can add images, guided maps, drawings, sticky notes, videos, shapes, and more (Miro, 2023).

Some pros of the Miro board include an easy-to-use interface for all users. With a link, all users can log on using the internet to collaborate and see up-to-date interactions. Miro also supports a variety of tasks such as brainstorming, collaboration, interactive meetings, lectures, organizing ideas, and more (Skubik-Peplaski et al., 2022). It is accessible to anyone who can log on to the internet. Miro has a way to add a timer, bring one or all students to where the conversation is located on the whiteboard, and celebrate success with their interactive buttons. Finally, it creates a differentiated approach to providing visualization tools for learners to increase learner presence (Skubik-Peplaski et al., 2022). Students shared that Miro was a way for them to stay engaged, collaborate with other students, and review and develop cognitive skills in a classroom (Thompson & Yuen, 2022).

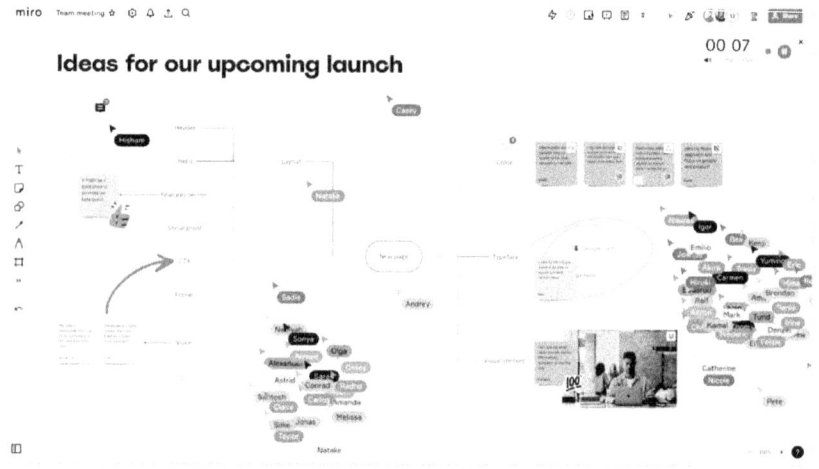

Figure 4: An example of how the Miro board can be used in an online classroom (Miro, 2023)

Some cons of the Miro board include the versatility of what the board provides and what can be done on the interactive whiteboard; this can be a learning curve for some individuals. The board requires stable internet and bandwidth, which might concern some people in a more rural area. Some students reported that it was sometimes hard to see where to post due to how big the whiteboard is (Johnson, 2022).

Overall, Miro is a great interactive tool that can be used in your online classroom or during meetings. With its ability to visually represent learners and team members, Miro is worth the cost of providing productivity and creativity in various educational environments.

Mentimeter

Mentimeter is a cloud-based online tool that can be used by large groups of participants (Fatemeh Ranjbaran Madiseh, 2022). Mentimeter is an online interactive platform similar to Poll Everywhere and Socrative that incorporates anonymous feedback during teaching (Vallely & Gibson, 2018). It keeps students engaged while assessing their knowledge and skills and creating a start to a discussion (Mentimeter, 2023). Mentimeter is similar to the clicker system without using clickers (Vallely & Gibson, 2018). Mentimeter provides a beneficial soundboard to start a seminar or lecture. It allows for a question to show up on the board and then individuals can answer, which allows for instant responses to provide guidance and direction for discussions (Vallely & Gibson, 2018). It allows for the fun and excitement of learning, similar to Kahoot (Vallely & Gibson, 2018).

The pros of Mentimeter include a more engaging way to assess a student's knowledge. Another pro would be the ability to see qualitatively and quantitatively where the students are academically (Vallely & Gibson, 2018). The platform is user-friendly and easy to learn and share during course instruction. Another advantage is that with the increase in instant feedback, educators can adjust their curriculum to meet the students where they are (Vallely & Gibson, 2018).

Some cons with Mentimeter include that the post is made anonymously, which means that the educator does not know which students are doing well and which ones are not (Vallely & Gibson, 2018). Students must also have a good internet connection to reply to the questions. Another con is that students cannot edit or view their responses once they have submitted them.

Overall, Mentimeter is a good online tool to help start a lecture or seminar and gain insight into where the students or audience are. It provides instant and anonymous responses to help educators gauge the direction they should go with their instruction or seminar.

Figure 5. An example of Mentimeter collage after a question was asked (Tips & Tricks July 2019 - Mentimeter & Padlet, 2019).

Flipgrid

Flipgrid is a video discussion forum that is designed to allow students to engage in a conversation with video and audio (Green & Green, 2018). Flipgrid can be used on a computer or on a mobile device. There are two main things with Flipgrid, including a grid that holds the classroom discussion and the topic of each discussion. Within each topic for discussion, multiple responses can be included (Green & Green, 2018). Flipgrid can be added to Canvas as a connection for the students to complete an assignment. To begin each conversation, the educator creates a topic for discussion to start the prompt, which can include a video or image. Students would then click on the big green plus sign to begin responding, which can be done live or with a previous video that was saved to the computer or other device (Green & Green, 2018).

The pros of using Flipgrid are that it is another tool to help analyze each student's knowledge and skills through discussions. It is another tool to provide an inclusive and differentiated approach to online learning. It is an easy-to-use online tool that any user should be able to figure out easily, and the students can also respond to each other's videos.

One of the cons of Flipgrid is that the students need the internet to participate in the discussion forum. If a student is an introvert, this may be challenging for them to do the assignment because they will have to listen and watch themselves speak. Flipgrid may have some technical issues that can cause some frustration with students wanting to get their assignments completed, and I noticed that it works better in Chrome than it does with Safari, and some students need to clear their internet cache as well to solve the technical issues.

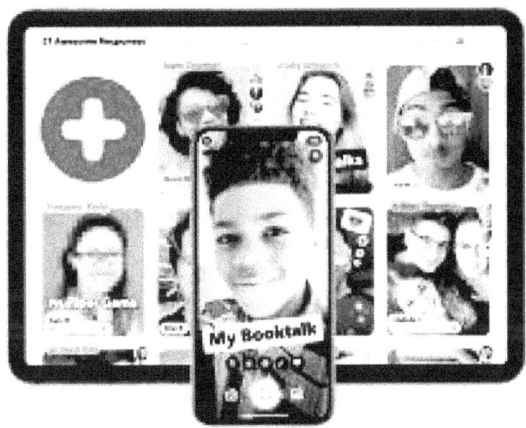

Figure 6: An example of how Flipgrid can look on a computer or a phone (Edwards, 2022).

Overall, Flipgrid is a fun and interactive way to add differentiated assignments to your classroom. It allows students to speak in a video with audio and for the teacher and other students to respond to their responses.

Canva

Another tool that is good to use as an educator in K–12 or higher education is Canva. Canva is a web-based graphic design platform that allows users to create various visual content, including flyers, posters, social media posts, announcements, certificates, and other graphics. They have a free and paid version with tools for beginners or more advanced designers for individuals, educators, or businesses. Canva was founded by Melanie Perkins, Cliff Obrecht, and Cameron Adams in 2012 (Gehred, 2020). Canva has many tools that can benefit many individuals, and we will share some of them below.

Canva offers a user interface that is easy and friendly to use for a variety of individuals. Canva offers an extensive library of designs, shapes, images, illustrations, icons, and fonts that can meet many users' needs (Gehred, 2020). Canva is offered in 190 countries and over 100 languages and works with all operating systems (Company, 2018; Gehred, 2020). In 2019, the company purchased free stock photo sites such as Pixabay and Pexels, which give users a variety of free photos for their graphic designs (Gehred, 2020). Canva continues to collaborate with illustrators, designers, and photographers worldwide to add to their library. This allows them to stay up-to-date with various design tools.

In conclusion, Canva is a wonderful design tool that makes it simple for many users to develop their designs for visualization, marketing, branding, educational purposes, and more. From being easy to use to adding graphics, making professional marketing materials, making email signatures and business cards, and adding Canvas headers, Canva has a variety of tools to help enhance a learning experience by making educational content more engaging.

Conclusion on Tools

Although COVID-19 was a shock to all individuals in the educational field and beyond, it set up more uses of technology, LMS, and other tools to help make classrooms more interactive and to promote a more mindful classroom, providing differentiating instruction for a diverse set of tools to help with student success. The online tools shared in this section of the series included Zoom, OWL, Miro board, Flipgrid, Padlet, Google Jamboard, Mentimeter, and Canva. All of these can be beneficial to providing a more engaging online classroom that is more student-centered and provides a more mindful experience.

References for Dr. Hind's Contribution:

Ali, A. (2021). Using Padlet as a Pedagogical Tool. *Journal of Learning Development in Higher Education*(22). https://doi.org/https://doi.org/10.47408/jldhe.vi22.799

Amin, E. (2020). A Review of Research into Google Apps in the Process of English Language Learning and Teaching. *Arab World English Journal*, *11*, 399-418. https://doi.org/10.24093/awej/vol11no1.27

Angeli, C. (2005). Preservice teachers as ICT designers: an instructional design model based on an expanded view of pedagogical content knowledge. J Comput-Assist Learn. *Journal of Computer Assisted Learning*, *21*, 292-302. https://doi.org/10.1111/j.1365-2729.2005.00135.x

Ching, Y.-H., Hsu, Y.-C., & Baldwin, S. (2018). Developing Computational Thinking with Educational Technologies for Young Learners. *TechTrends*, *62*(6), 563-573. https://doi.org/10.1007/s11528-018-0292-7

Company, F. (2018). *Locker M. Graphic design startup Canva just turned into a unicorn.*

Edwards, L. (2022). *What is Flip and How Does it Work for Teachers and Students? Tips and Tricks*. Retrieved July 12 from https://www.techlearning.com/how-to/what-is-flipgrid-and-how-does-it-work-for-teachers-and-students

Fatemeh Ranjbaran Madiseh, A. A. A., Hadi Sobhanifar et al. . (2022). Integration of Mentimeter into the Classroom: A Scoping Review. *Research Square* https://doi.org/10.21203/rs.3.rs-1339347/v1

Gehred, A. P. (2020). Canva. *Journal of the Medical Library Association : JMLA*, *108(2)*, 338–340. https://doi.org/https://doi.org/10.5195/jmla.2020.940

Green, T., & Green, J. (2018). Flipgrid: Adding Voice and Video to Online Discussions. *TechTrends*, *62*(1), 128-130. https://doi.org/10.1007/s11528-017-0241-x

Heflin, H., & Macaluso, S. (2021). Student Initiative Empowers Engagementfor Learning Online. *Online Learning*, *25*(3), 230-248. https://doi.org/10.24059/olj.v25i3.2414

Hinds, J. A., & Johns, B. H. (2023). Stress Performance Evaluation (SPE) Is a Novel Method of Measuring Physiological Responsiveness to Testing in Children with a Learning Disability. *Education Sciences*, *13*(6), 594. https://www.mdpi.com/2227-7102/13/6/594

Hinds, J. A., & Sanchez, E. R. (2022). The Role of the Hypothalamus–Pituitary–Adrenal (HPA) Axis in Test-Induced Anxiety: Assessments, Physiological Responses, and Molecular Details. *Stresses*, *2*(1), 146-155. https://www.mdpi.com/2673-7140/2/1/11

Hodges, T. S., Kerch, C., & Fowler, M. . (2020). Teacher Education in the Time of COVID-19: Creating Digital Networks as University-School-Family Partnerships. *Middle Grades Review*,, *6*(2). https://doi.org/ https://scholarworks.uvm.edu/mgreview/vol6/iss2/4

Houston, D., Meyer, L. H., & Paewai, S. (2006). Academic Staff Workloads and Job Satisfaction: Expectations and values in academe. *Journal of Higher Education Policy and Management*, *28*(1), 17-30. https://doi.org/10.1080/13600800500283734

Inc, Z. (2016). Security guide. Zoom Video Communications Inc. *Retrieved October*, *9*, 2020.

Jamboard Reviews. (2023). https://www.softwareadvice.com/whiteboard/jamboard-profile/reviews/

Johnson, E. K. (2022). *Miro, Miro: Student perceptions of a visual discussion board* Proceedings of the 40th ACM International Conference on Design of Communication, Boston, MA, USA. https://doi.org/10.1145/3513130.3558983

Kali, Y., Goodyear, P., & Markauskaite, L. (2011). Researching design practices and design cognition: Contexts, experiences and pedagogical knowledge-in-pieces. *Learning, Media and Technology*, *36*, 129-149. https://doi.org/10.1080/17439884.2011.553621

Khoiriyah, K., Kairoty, N., & Aljasysyarin, A. (2022). The use of Google Jamboard for synchronous collaborative reading strategies: The students' acceptance. *VELES Voice of English Language Education Society*, *6*, 52-66. https://doi.org/10.29408/veles.v6i1.5010

Labs, O. (2023). *Meeting OWL 3*. Retrieved July 10 from

Mentimeter. (2023). *Make Your Teaching Count*. Retrieved July 14 from https://www.mentimeter.com/

Miro. (2023). *Miro as your whiteboard tool*. Retrieved July 12 from https://miro.com/whiteboard/

Navarro, M. C. (2021). *What is Jamboard: Using the Digital Whiteboard in a Hybrid Classroom*. Retrieved July 14 from https://vibe.us/blog/how-to-use-jamboard/

Nesher Shoshan, H., & Wehrt, W. (2022). Understanding "Zoom fatigue": A mixed-method approach. *Applied Psychology*, *71*(3), 827-852. https://doi.org/https://doi.org/10.1111/apps.12360

Robinson, G. (2020). *4 fantastic uses for Padlet in online teaching*. University of Sussex. Retrieved July 12 from https://blogs.sussex.ac.uk/tel/2020/07/28/4-fantastic-uses-for-padlet-in-online-teaching/

Skubik-Peplaski, C., Edick, J., & Cook, W. (2022). Agile learning and teaching with miro boards.

Thompson, A., & Yuen, B. (2022). Using Miro to Enhance Students' Online Engagement and Learning in a Science Communication Module.

Tips & Tricks July 2019 - Mentimeter & Padlet. (2019). Retrieved July 14 from https://promote.zendesk.com/hc/en-us/articles/360008032040-Tips-Tricks-July-2019-Mentimeter-Padlet

Vallely, K. S. A., & Gibson, P. F. (2018). Engaging students on their devices with Mentimeter. *Compass: Journal of Learning and Teaching*.

Veletsianos, G., & Houlden, S. (2020). Radical Flexibility and Relationality as Responses to Education in Times of Crisis. *Postdigital Science and Education*, *2*(3), 849-862. https://doi.org/10.1007/s42438-020-00196-3